THE WORKING DEAD

STEVE BURNS

HOLLY BURNS

PREFACE

We wrote this book during the winter of 2019, just months before the COVID-19 pandemic began ravaging our planet. We agonized for weeks over whether we should delay the release of the book. As I write this introduction, almost two million people have become infected and the death toll across the globe is devastating. The US has exceeded 500,000 cases and more than 20,000 people have lost their battle with the virus. And they tell us the worst is yet to come.

We decided to publish the book because we think the principles contained here changed our lives, and may ultimately save our lives. Let me explain. Several years ago, we sold our house and downsized our belongings so we could move out of the city. We were ready for a slower pace and dedicated to living a simpler life in the country. We bought a home surrounded by beautiful hardwood trees and farmland, and were finally living the dream and enjoying life on our own terms.

Now the peaceful setting and slow pace seem less important than population density and our ability to stay home and practice social distancing. Our financial freedom also means that we've been better insulated against the sharp economic downturn the pandemic has caused. None of this would have been possible without the principles that we follow and share in this book.

There may be a better time to release this book, but maybe not. We don't know what the future holds, but we do know that what we share here has helped us achieve financial independence, and that freedom may end up saving us both physically and financially. We wanted to share it with you.

Holly Burns
April 2020

INTRODUCTION

"If you don't find a way to make money while you sleep, you will work until you die." - Warren Buffett

---

Financial freedom can be described as an individual or household having enough money to live on without depending on income from an employer.

This book isn't written for people working their dream job, or those unwilling to evaluate the time and money spent on items that aren't likely to bring them long-term happiness. If you're obsessed with owning the biggest house, driving the newest car or using your credit cards to take lavish vacations, this book probably isn't for you. Likewise, this book doesn't tell you how to get rich quick. Instead, it explains principles you can use to become fiscally responsible, self-sufficient and brave enough to be your own boss.

There's nothing wrong with enjoying the finer things, but it's important that you acquire items and experiences as you can afford them; you make your life unnecessarily difficult if you try to live like a millionaire by taking on debt. You're unlikely to *be* wealthy if you leverage every penny you make to *appear* wealthy.

The good news is that obtaining financial freedom isn't as difficult as it may seem. If you start making plans to be self-sufficient, you'll give yourself a wonderful gift, time. With time on your side, you can invest in yourself, build profitable assets and reach your financial goals.

Financial independence is having enough money to walk away from your job and do something you're passionate about every day. Instead of giving someone 40 hours a week, 50 weeks a year, you can reclaim your time and spend it however you choose.

This book will help you earn more, keep more of what you earn and explain how to put that money to work for you. In the following pages we'll explore principles of financial independence. These principles are broken down into four categories.

- Financial Future
- Low Stress Finances
- Building Wealth
- Financial Freedom

Holly and I have been fortunate enough to share our passion with each other and our readers and students, and now we're excited to share the principles that helped us become financially independent and achieve our dreams.

Steve Burns

I

FINANCIAL FUTURE

1

YOUR GOALS

"If you don't know where you are going, any road will get you there." - Lewis Carroll

Written goals are powerful tools that can help you achieve your long-term hopes and dreams. They can focus your daily, monthly and yearly energy on the actions that will help you achieve success. It's important that you decide what you want your future to look like, and then follow a plan to get there. Here are a few questions that will help you pinpoint your financial goals.

- How much do you want to earn?
- What would you do if you could do anything?
- Do you have any hobbies that you can turn into a business or cash flowing assets?
- Do you want to own a business that you own/operate, or do you prefer cash flowing assets?
- Are big houses and fancy cars important to you?

- Do you want to focus on increasing earning power or being as frugal as possible?
- Where do you want to live? Are you okay in a rural area, or do you need to live in a large city?
- Do you want to be an employee, business owner, investor or trader?
- What type of business do you want to work in, own or invest in?
- What do you spend money on that brings you the most joy?
- What's the most important thing to you? Optimizing your life for happiness, peace of mind, growing your wealth, advancing your career or providing for your family?

I wrote my first goals in the margin of a book on the topic when I was 19, and I've continued this habit throughout my lifetime. I'm starting the book with this principle because I know that it's one of the most important aspects of success. Remember, having a target doesn't mean you'll hit it, but if you don't have a target, you're guaranteed to miss it. Here are some thoughts on goal setting for your to consider.

- How can you achieve success if you don't know what that looks like?
- Writing down your financial goals helps you visualize what you want and give you focus.
- Before every significant decision, ask yourself whether what you're contemplating will move you closer or farther away from your financial goals.
- If you consistently strive to achieve your goals, even if you need to course correct along the way, you're likely to get there in the end.

- Only time separates you from achieving your goals if you're dedicated and hard working.
- Writing down your financial goals will help you decide if you're willing to do what it takes to get what you want.

If your goal is financial independence, then you need to figure out what it will take to make that happen. Start from the endpoint and work backwards. In order to leave your job and be self-sufficient, you'll need to have enough cash flowing assets to pay your bills and replace your paycheck, or a net worth large enough to support you for the rest of your life. In the latter case, remember that the spending rate of your capital must be less than the capital appreciation through interest, dividends or capital gains. In other words, you can't spend more than you make because you have a fixed income.

Financial freedom is just math, and in the following pages we'll be discussing two concepts that will help you achieve your financial goals; earning power and financial defense. By focusing on earning power, you'll build the wealth you need to be self-sufficient. Financial defense will limit the amount of money you lose, and keep your wealth intact for a lifetime. After all, it doesn't do much good to achieve your dream of being financially independent if you eventually have to return to the grind!

Financial freedom begins when you determine what your ideal future looks like, and you create a written plan to make that dream a reality.

2

YOUR PURPOSE

"Choose a job you love and you will never have to work a day in your life." - Oriental proverb

Why do most people work at a certain job? They likely took a job because it was available, they knew someone that worked there, or their family gave them a leg-up. Few people mindfully choose what they do for a living. Too many young people go to college because they feel like they're *supposed to*, without any idea what they want to do long-term. In fact, college is setup for people to take general courses first, while they decide what degree they eventually want to pursue. It's not unusual for students to change their mind and major before graduation.

Children that start pursuing their lifelong passion in sports or music when they're five years old have a decade of experience over 15-year-olds that are just starting out. History's great successes from Mozart to Tiger Woods didn't get a job, they chose a lifelong passion and pursued it relentlessly from childhood.

We all have something that we've been drawn to in life; games we played as a child, creative hobbies, or a particular career path. Ask yourself what you would do every day if money didn't matter? When you can answer that question, you can design a lifestyle that reflects your dreams. Rather than trying to squeeze in time for what makes you happy on your two week vacation from the job you dislike, you'll be able to do what makes you happy every day and be paid for it.

It's never been easier to monetize a passion. The barrier to entry has been lowered across every industry thanks to platforms like YouTube, Shopify, WordPress, Amazon and Etsy. And if you're interested in trading and investing, you now have access to zero commission investing and trading. There's literally *nothing* holding you back.

If you're working a job you dislike and you can't breakaway immediately due to your responsibilities and debt, don't give up. Your current situation doesn't have to be your final disposition. If you're currently working for someone else, focus on a career path or skill set that will increase earning power long-term. Companies will often pay for continuing education related to your job, and this can be a good way to increase your skills, experience and income.

If you've positioned yourself in an industry you're interested in, you'll be setting yourself up to start your own business with the skills, experience and capital necessary to do so. The sooner you can start getting paid for doing what you love, the easier it will be to achieve financial freedom, because you'll have the passion necessary to do the work required to be successful.

We have more flexibility and opportunity when we're young. We don't have large mortgages, expensive car payments, credit card debt, or spouses and children that we're responsible for. As we get older and take on more debt and responsibility, our time decreases and we have fewer opportunities to follow our dreams. If we do what we love from the start, our lives will be simpler, happier and more fulfilling.

Here are a few things you can do if you find yourself trapped in a job you dislike.

- Create a plan for financial independence with a specific achievement date.
- Limit the time you stay in your job by maximizing earnings and minimizing spending. Not only will you see a light at the end of the tunnel, but you'll have a greater sense of purpose.
- Start saving and/or investing aggressively. Put savings into the stock market or high yielding bonds to quickly increase your net worth.
- Start a side business. Do you have a skill you can sell to customers or clients? Can you monetize any of your hobbies? Can you use a monetize a platform like Amazon, Etsy, eBay, Thumbtack, Takl, etc.?
- Can you create digital cash flowing assets like websites, books, eBooks, audio books or eCourses?
- Have you thought about a cash flowing business like rental properties, vending machines, car washes or laundromats?

Find something you're passionate about and then find a way to make money doing it. If you're going to spend 40-50 hours a week working, you may as well spend that time on your passion instead of someone else's.

Being financially free means you can get up every day and do what brings meaning and purpose to your life. If you love what you do, then you're already on your way to financial freedom. If you dislike what you do, then it's time to start developing your exit strategy.

3

_____

YOUR GROWTH

The best pay you can receive from a job is in experience, knowledge, connections and opportunity.

There are many ways to learn, and here are a few to consider. You can go to a higher learning institution and be taught by professors. You can start at an entry level position in your chosen profession to gain valuable experience; adjusting and improving based on feedback and success. You can find a knowledgable mentor to help guide you towards your goals. You may decide that the knowledge you need can be learned through books or eCourses developed by successful people in your chosen field.

Never underestimate the power of a long-term goal based on your passion. There's a significant psychological difference between working in a restaurant for an hourly wage, and using your love of food to become a chef or restauranteur.

How much you grow personally from a job is more important

than the paycheck you receive. Interns work for free to acquire experience and make connections in the field they're interested in. Networking is an important and oftentimes overlooked part of any job. Most job openings will be filled by someone that the employer already knows or a current employee recommends. Any paid job you take needs to teach you new skills, let you practice the skills you have, or give you the potential for significant income to meet your financial goals faster.

Many successful people have accepted a mentor's knowledge as payment. Billionaire money manager, Paul Tudor Jones, got coffee and answered phones all day for a trader when he started out. Everyone has to start somewhere, and you should start with someone who's already been where you're trying to go.

There may be no better way to learn than by doing. If you goal is to be an author, you can start writing blogs or publishing eBooks, reading reviews and looking at sales data. Based on your observations, you can make adjustments and do more of what works and less of what doesn't. It's critical that you critique your results and make adjustments, because someone with 10-years of experience may be no better than a rookie if they never learn from their mistakes.

Books are an affordable way to learn from an established expert while reducing the learning curve. Some of your best options will be autobiographies or biographies that aggregate the principles of successful millionaires, traders, investors, CEOs and entrepreneurs in your chosen field. Remember, books can give you valuable knowledge and a shortcut, but only you can do the work necessary for success.

eCourses are also effective learning tools because they can deliver information from an established expert in a multimedia format. By adding visual aids, sound and step-by-step examples, some learners will find them easier to understand and more enjoyable.

Do you need a college degree? It depends on your ultimate goal. A degree for some professions, but if you need to learn specific skills like a programming language, business practices or creative writing, you may decide to take only the classes that directly impact your long-term goals.

4

YOUR LIFE PARTNER

"I, ____, take you, ____, to be my lawfully wedded (husband/wife), to have and to hold, from this day forward, for better, for worse, for richer, for poorer, in sickness and in health, until death do us part." - Catholic wedding vows

Most people don't associate love with financial freedom, but your choice of a life partner will be one of the most important financial decisions you make. Staying single decreases your risk of financial ruin, but marrying the right person can double your income and increase your chances of financial success.

Many people say that you can't control who you love, but you can control who's in your life. You owe it to yourself to make sure that the person you give your heart to won't lead you both down a path of financial ruin. Finding someone who shares your goal of being financially independent should be a top priority. If your long-term goal is to pay off your debt and work for yourself, you'll have a difficult time achieving those goals with someone who's a hyper-consumer. If you think keeping up with the Joneses is tough, you'll find that marrying someone who sets the pace for the neighborhood is a nightmare.

If you marry a high-earner and they spend more than they make or require constant upgrades in one form or another, you'll have a difficult time getting off the hamster wheel of earning and spending. Even worse, if they love to spend but hate to earn, they can create a downward spiral that leads to financial ruin.

Fifty percent of all marriages end in divorce, likely because they got married for the wrong reasons or chose to marry the wrong person. Many people fall into the same trap with their marriage that they do with their job; they marry someone they know or someone recommended by someone they know. It's going to take a lot more than liking someone or being attracted to them to be happy for a life-time. It's important to look outside your circle of friends and coworkers to find someone who shares your goals, priorities and dreams. Marrying the wrong person can result in a divorce, and the cost of these are usually devastating, both emotionally and financially.

When you do find the right life partner, make their happiness your number one priority. Dedicate yourself to maintaining good communication and meeting their needs, and never take them for granted. Your long-term happiness will pay you dividends in many ways. In addition to a wonderful quality of life, you're likely to see financial rewards for your long-term commitment. According to a study by the National Bureau of Economic Research, retirement age couples have nearly ten times the financial assets of singles. A happy and successful marriage can be your greatest asset.

5

YOUR PERCEIVED WORTH

"Surplus value is equal to the new value created by workers in excess of their own labor-costs, which is appropriated by the capitalist by profits when products are sold." - Karl Marx

Financial markets are efficient at pricing labor inside existing business models. When a business does a poor job of labor pricing, it manifests as unfilled job positions or high turnover. If a company says they can't find good employees, they're probably not paying well enough, and the employees they do have are likely searching for better pay somewhere else. The best employees already have jobs, but people will often change companies for the right pay and benefits.

People become frustrated when they see professional sports stars and actors making millions while teachers and soldiers make much less. Pay isn't based on morals, opinions or feelings, it's based on economics. Supply and demand set pay rates, not someone's opinion about fairness.

If a professional athlete can pack a stadium and lead their team to a championship, then the owner will pay for the value added to their franchise. A movie studio will pay an actor who can pack a movie theater and make them millions of dollars. Despite how valuable and essential they are, teachers and soldiers make less money because there are many more of them in the system. This means that regardless of what's fair, employers are able to pay them less and offer fewer benefits.

In a properly functioning job market, wages naturally move to an equilibrium of supply and demand, the positions are filled and the turnover is minimal. If pay doesn't attract workers, there's a shortage of employees. If wages are high, there's a large number of applicants competing for the same job.

While working towards financial freedom, your income should be based on the value and profit you create for your employer. The more value you can bring, the more pay you should receive, and the faster you can become financially independent.

6

YOUR NET WORTH

Your current net worth is the difference between the monetary value you've created and your consumption of goods, products and services. It's a reflection of your ability to make good financial decisions.

Your net worth is what you have after you subtract your liabilities from your assets.

Potential assets:

- Home value
- Taxable investment portfolio
- Tax deferred 401K, 403B or IRA
- Property
- Checking account balance
- Savings account
- Equity in your car
- Business valuation

- Collectables
- Websites
- Intellectual property
- Loans that you have given
- Items you own

Potential liabilities:

- Mortgage
- Second mortgage
- Home equity line of credit
- Student loans
- Car loans
- Credit cards
- Personal loans
- Bill consolidation loans
- Investment account margin
- Boat loans
- Motorcycle loans

Add the value of the things you own and subtract the debt you owe. The difference between these values is your current net worth.

Here's a simple example:

Assets:

- Home value $300,000
- Investments $50,000
- Savings $4,000
- Checking $1,000

Total asset value: $355,000

Liabilities:

- Mortgage $250,000

- Student loans $100,000
- Car loans $25,000
- Credit Card debt $10,000

Liabilities: $385,000

In this example $355,000 - $385,000 equals - $30,000 resulting in a negative net worth. This is typical in many households, especially when someone is just starting out. Here's another example:

Assets:

- Home value $350,000
- Individual Retirement Accounts $250,000
- Investments $50,000
- Savings $10,000
- Checking $5,000

Total asset value: $665,000

Liabilities:

- Mortgage $100,000

In this example $665,000 - $100,000 equals - $565,000, resulting in a positive net worth of more than half a million dollars. This household worked hard to control spending and made saving and investing a priority.

Growing net worth gives you peace of mind and opens up more opportunities for financial freedom. It's important to calculate your net worth to see how you're doing so you can make changes for your financial future.

7

YOUR BUDGET

A budget is a written financial plan that quantifies the earning and spending discipline necessary for financial well-being.

An important aspect of financial freedom is spending, and a budget is a great way to track your spending habits. A monthly budget is a written plan that promotes responsible spending, acting as a tool to identify and address financial issues in a condensed period of time.

If you consistently exceed your monthly budget, you may determine that you have an earning issue. You could close the gap by increasing your income with a promotion, second job or a higher paying job. If this isn't possible and you see that you have a spending problem, you'll be able to identify the problem category and act quickly to change spending habits.

Make a monthly budget by writing down your take-home income and all the bills you have during the month. Include things that may not be a physical bill, like money for lunch or parking, etc. Make sure you take into account the frequency of your income and the due dates of your bills. Are you making enough to cover everything? Do you have money leftover that you can invest or put into savings? Should you think about increasing your income?

Do a recap at the end of the month to see what you *really* spent and what, if any, areas you need to address. The next step is to project your income and your plan into the next month to see what you should plan for in the future. This is a simple example, but even taking these first steps can help you on your path to financial independence.

It's interesting that in Thomas Stanley's best-selling book, "The Millionaire Next Door," those interviewed had significantly different views on budgeting. Some of them kept detailed budgets, while other millionaires were disciplined and never used them at all. You may not need a budget if you have a high income and live frugally. However, if you or your partner have a problem with both earning *and* spending, a budget can be an important tool to identify those issues, expedite paying off debt and avoid temptations like credit cards.

Credit cards can act as an important safety net to avoid financial ruin, but they should never be used as a crutch to purchase things you couldn't afford otherwise. You may need to employ the Cash Only system if you find it difficult to live within your means. At the beginning of your budget period, take out the cash you can afford to spend and when it's gone, it's gone. This doesn't have to be a permanent solution, but it can help you learn good spending habits.

8

YOUR COST

"The cost of a thing is the amount of what I will call life, which is required to be exchanged for it, immediately or in the long run." - Henry David Thoreau

---

Have you ever thought about whether your job is worth it? Jobs aren't free. They cost time, energy and lost opportunities. They limit your ability to spend time with family and friends, and rarely leave you with enough energy to do something for yourself.

Jobs are more than pay. Do you like working for your boss? Do you like the company you work for? Do you love the work you do? If you make good money and enjoy your job, good for you! You're in the lucky minority, and you can focus on fiscal health and your eventual retirement. If you don't like your job, your boss or the company you work for, your employment may be costing you more than you think. Here are a few costs to consider.

- The cost of a college education to be qualified for your job
- Commuting costs like gasoline, car maintenance, car depreciation, car insurance, etc.
- Getting take-out when you're too tired to cook
- Unpaid time spent commuting to and from your job
- Childcare costs
- Income taxes
- Wardrobe and/or dry cleaning costs
- Health care costs when physical or emotional issues take their toll
- Unsuccessful relationships/divorce

Some may seem extreme or you haven't encountered them, while others will be all too familiar. Jobs are how most people make a living and take care of their families, but it's important to realize that they do have a cost. It's essential that you find a job you like or find a way to work for yourself doing something you love.

There are many things to think about, like the distance to your job, the need for childcare, the increase in tax brackets if you earn more, etc. Having a high paying job may seem like it's worth it, but do the math and make sure. A job should value your time and energy, compensate you fairly for your efforts and make you happy every payday.

If you're not getting paid for your efforts or you're constantly unhappy, is any amount of money worth your happiness and health? If you don't love what you do, it's time to make a change. Make your part-time job finding a new full-time job or creating your own dream job.

9

YOUR VALUE

"One of the enemies of happiness is adaptation. We buy things to make us happy, and we succeed. But only for awhile. New things are exciting to us at first, but then we adapt to them." - Dr. Gilovich

The hedonic treadmill is about new cars, bigger houses and increasing salaries. And while these may seem desirable, objects can't make us happy over the long-term. The tendency is to quickly return to the previous level of contentment, regardless of positive or negative life events. As someone makes more money, their expectations and desires rise to meet the new income level. This creates higher expectations and greater stress. Happiness and contentment don't necessarily coincide with these psychological increases.

It's a good idea to ask yourself if an upcoming purchase will bring you closer to your financial goals. Everyone will have a different answers to this question. Personally, when I spend money on something that saves me time, like lawn care service, I feel like I'm getting incredible value for my money. By allocating time to the person with the right skills for the job, whether they work for you directly or you employ their services, you're using resources wisely.

Focus on paying people to do the things you don't like to do so you can focus on things that will bring you closer to your financial goals. Both parties will benefit from it and you'll be improving your quality of life in the process. Your quality of life is a better investment than spending money on depreciating items.

Let's look at a car purchase as an example. If your car (a depreciating asset) payment is $800 a month, are you getting twice the enjoyment or quality of life improvement over a $400 a month car? Would your lower stress level be worth driving a car that's paid for? Again, different people will have different desires and needs. Some people are car lovers and it's a top priority for them. Others may not want to own a car at all, preferring to use public transportation or ride sharing services like Uber and Lyft.

Some people love to own things and it's the driving force behind their decision making process. For others, financial health and not being trapped in a job they dislike is their top priority. There's nothing wrong with owning things that you want and can afford. But if you want to be financially independent, being leveraged by large debt can significantly limit your options. Large mortgages, car payments, student loans and credit card debt will curtail your ability to leave your job and do something you want to do. Only you can decide what's more important to you.

Experiences offer the greatest value for your money. Focus on creating memories that will last a lifetime, or utilizing services that will increase your daily enjoyment. Your Netflix subscription may give you more entertainment every month than one trip to the movies, and a budget family vacation close to home is likely to give you the same wonderful memories as an expensive 7-day cruise.

Money can buy consumer goods, experiences, comfort, convenience, travel, technology and luxury, but it can also buy the freedom to do what you want with your time. The value you get from something should always be worth the money you spend, and make sure to factor in the time and energy required to earn that money.

10

YOUR PASSION

"Take the job you would take if you were independently wealthy. You're going to do well at it." - Warren Buffett

A rich businessman went on vacation to a beach resort in the Caribbean. Each day, he sat on the beach and watched a local fisherman in a small boat reel in fish. At the end of every day, the fisherman took his catch to the local seafood market and got paid just enough to get by. In the evening, he would walk to the beachside bar and relax with his friends.

The businessman watched the fisherman day after day and contemplated the mistakes the fisherman was making. He decided it was his duty to educate the fisherman before he returned home, so he approached him on the beach the next day.

"I see you out here every day, and I'd like to share some business advice with you."

The fisherman looked puzzled.

"I notice that you only fish for two hours a day. If you fished for four hours a day you could double your income," explained the businessman.

"Why would I do that?"

"Well, so you could make enough money to buy a bigger boat," the businessman replied.

The fisherman frowned.

"Why would I need a bigger boat?"

"To increase your capacity. If you buy a bigger boat and increase your capacity you can expand your business. You can buy more boats, hire people to fish for you and increase your revenue. You could develop your brand, and one day go public or sell it for a handsome profit!" The businessman smiled.

"Why would I want to be rich?"

"Because you could do whatever you want to do! What would you do if you had the money to do anything you wanted?" the businessman asked.

"Well, I guess I would live on the beach in the Caribbean, fish for a couple hours a day, drink a beer on the beach with my friends, and then go spend time with my family."

Start with the end goal in mind. Think about what you would do if you had unlimited money or money didn't matter. If you could do anything, what would it be? What would your lifestyle look like? Some of the richest people in the world continue to work long after they need to because they enjoy what they do. Steve Jobs, Jeff Bezos and Warren Buffett are good examples. In fact, Steve Jobs was already a billionaire many times over before he inspired Apple to create the iPhone.

Money isn't the best barometer for determining what you should do for a living. A better metric is the passion you have for a particular subject. If you can get up every morning and be excited about your job, your business or your investments, you have a significant advantage over people dragging themselves out of bed to do something they dislike. Your passion will translate into drive and that drive will keep you focused and dedicated, while others will seek distractions to alleviate their stress and unhappiness.

It's difficult to excel in a job you dislike. Most people can tough it out for a while, but success comes from working at the same thing until you master it, and that takes a long time. The only way to stay focused, have enough energy to work through the learning curve and become successful, is with passion.

II

LOW STRESS FINANCES

11

YOUR EARNING POWER

Buy what you can't afford and you'll stay trapped in a job you don't like.

The greater the gap between earning power and debt, the more financial pressure you'll experience. Paying monthly bills and having money left over to save, invest or build a business can give you a financial cushion and alleviate stress.

Acquiring debt by continuously spending more than you make is dangerous, and the main contributor of this vicious cycle is compounding interest. If you can't pay cash for what you buy or you can't pay off your credit cards at the end of the month, you'll start paying interest on the debt you can't afford. This is a slippery slope that takes you farther from financial freedom and sets you up for possible financial ruin.

Personal finance shouldn't cause you stress. Stress is a warning sign; it's the mind's way of telling your body that you're in danger.

Purchases should make you feel positive and secure, not worried that you won't be able to pay for them if something goes wrong.

An important part of financial freedom is learning to say no to yourself and others. Having the discipline to say no to yourself or family members when you can't afford something, will save money and reduce stress on your personal relationships.

Money is still the number one stressor in a relationship, and it only gets worse the deeper you go into debt. Knowing what you can and can't afford is important, but having the discipline to say no to yourself and others will determine your financial well-being.

Many entrepreneurs starting out make lifestyle sacrifices. They sleep on a friend's couch, eat peanut butter sandwiches and skip nights out on the town. New bands share apartments and vehicles to save money, and there are many hopeful actors in New York and Hollywood waiting tables. They make these sacrifices because they've put their dreams first. They haven't bought houses and new cars or overspent on credit cards, because they wouldn't be able to maintain that lifestyle while pursuing their dreams. Achieving their goal is their number one priority.

The more money you have left after paying your bills, the less stress you'll have. But earning a lot of money isn't necessarily the answer, because you can't out earn hyper-consumerism. Spending will always rise to meet the earning power. Good examples of this are the entertainers, sports stars and lottery winners who spent every-thing they made and had to file for bankruptcy. Your financial freedom is based on your ability to earn *and* your level of self-control.

12

MURPHY'S LAW

"The chance of the bread falling with the buttered side down is directly proportional to the cost of the carpet." - Murphy's Law

S hit happens, that's the nature of the world. Things wear down, age and break. We age, and at some point we'll likely have health related expenses. You'll have less financial stress if you keep enough money in reserve to handle unexpected expenses. Being ready for an emergency pays dividends in peace of mind, and reaching for your savings account is a lot less painful than reaching for your credit card in the long run.

Don't worry about the interest or returns on your savings account. Think about how you'll feel knowing that you can handle a car breakdown, a medical emergency or an unexpected house repair. That peace of mind is worth whatever you had to give up to save money.

Look for opportunities to pad your emergency fund every chance you get. Don't immediately buy a new car when you pay off the old one. Instead, divert that all or part of that money to your savings account. If you get a raise at work, increase the monthly savings amount without adding debt. Always choose self-control over self-indulgence, it will benefit you in the end.

Having a large stress-free fund can also lower monthly insurance premiums, because you can raise your deductible on your house, car or medical insurance. You'll pay less every month and increase how much you can save, and you can cover the deductible gap should you need to.

Resist the urge to buy the 'micro insurance' policies that they try to sell on everything from laptops to toasters. They make a fortune on the policies, and while it may not seem like much at the register, they can add up over time. Remember, you won't need to worry about your purchases breaking because you'll be putting the money you save from those policies into your savings account.

Savings accounts aren't about returns on capital, they're about peace of mind.

13

GROWING WEALTH

Debt should only be used as a tool to control assets, and even then, proceed with caution.

Borrowing money to buy physical items that depreciate in value isn't the path to financial health. However, it's possible to gain wealth by leveraging someone else's money to purchase items that increase in value. The key is choosing investments that increase in value rather than depreciating assets.

Don't buy a car that decreases in value and worth a fraction of the purchase price when it's paid off, invest in a rental property that generates cash flow each month and increases in value over time. Consumer debt destroys capital, while leveraged investments can grow wealth.

Debt can be used for assets that generate cash flow, increase in value or both. Popular forms of debt are new car loans, credit card debt, home equity loans and 30-year mortgages. These rarely produce wealth or lead to financial freedom. In contrast, real estate loans for rental properties or house flipping, small business loans to start or grow a business and loans to acquire cash flowing assets can build wealth. Most wealthy people have learned to leverage debt to increase their net worth.

As we've discussed before, it's important to consider whether a four year college degree is necessary to meet your life goals, because it can be a significant amount of debt to take on. Many people graduating from traditional universities with six-figure college loan debt will struggle for years to repay the expense. If your long-term goal is financial independence and you take on a large amount of debt before you get started, you're guaranteeing that you'll be selling your time to an employer for years or decades.

Many people will hesitate to take out a small business loan or take on debt to buy cash flowing assets. There's risk involved, but there's also risk in consumer debt if you're working for someone else and you lose your earning potential. You should determine your maximum risk tolerance by thinking of your worst case scenario and decide if you could come back from the loss.

Debt is about mindset and goals. The same people who cringe when thinking about taking out a small business loan wouldn't think twice about using credit cards on vacation. It makes more sense to invest in a business in the hopes of a return on investment rather than buying a new car to drive to a job, or spending money on a cruise to get away from that job.

Debt isn't good or bad, it's a tool that can be used to accomplish financial goals. All debt has risks, and how well you understand and manage those risks will influence your success.

14

F-YOU MONEY

F-you money is a get out of jail free card when your job feels like a prison.

Having money independent of another person's control gives you the freedom to walk away from bad bosses, bad jobs and customers that aren't worth your time and energy. Even more importantly, it can create incredible opportunities.

If you hate your job and you have enough money, you can leave that job and focus on finding one you love. If you dislike where you live, you can move somewhere else. F-you money empowers you to make decisions about your future that most people only dream about. Those decisions will shape your life and directly impact your happiness and the happiness of those around you.

F-you money equates to the length of time that you can live between income streams without acquiring debt. That kind of money gives you the ability to fire your boss, end unhealthy relationships, take control of your life and empowers you to say *no*. It means that you do what you want to do, in a healthy and appreciative environment, for the financial compensation that you think is appropriate. It allows you to buy back your time and focus on the things that make you happy.

One of the first steps on the path to financial freedom is the ability to walk away from jobs, people and circumstances you aren't happy with. F-you money unlocks the cage door and sets you free.

PAY YOURSELF FIRST

If you don't pay yourself first, who are you working for?

Whether you're utilizing a written budget or using self-control, the first person you should pay is yourself. Wealth comes from investing, buying or creating appreciating assets or starting a business. To do any of these things, you'll need investment capital, and one of the best ways to acquire capital is to actively save the difference between what you make and what you spend.

A savings account should be set aside with a specific goal, like moving it into a brokerage account for investing, or into a checking account to purchase an asset or invest in a business. The money you've allotted for your savings account should be transferred *before* you make any purchases or have any discretionary spending.

If you aren't paying yourself first, your cash will make other people wealthy and you'll struggle to find financial freedom.

- Employees make their bosses wealthy

- Debtors make banks wealthy
- Consumers make business owners wealthy
- Renters make their landlords wealthy
- Bonuses make executives wealthy

Start implementing a 10% saving process as soon as possible. Setup an automatic withdrawal from your checking account to your savings account. If you make $1,000 a week, setup your account to automatically move $100 into your savings. Another strategy is to contribute to your company's 401K program. If they match up to 5% of your contribution, deduct 5% from your pay automatically and your savings will double with half the effort.

However you decide to reward yourself for a job well done, if you don't making paying yourself a priority, no one else will. Your money will come and go without anything to show for it, and you'll miss opportunities because you don't have investment capital. By paying yourself first, you increase your chances (and speed up the process) of being financially independent.

16

USING YOUR MONEY

Your money should be used as a tool to make more money.

Having cash on hand to cover financial emergencies is important, but that isn't an accurate measure of wealth. Modern-day money isn't backed by gold or silver, it's a fiat currency. The dollar's value is a note of exchange for all public and private debt, backed only by the good faith of the US government and the military.

The world's currencies are valued against each other, which is demonstrated in foreign exchange rates and forex currency markets. Central banks of the world create perceived value by controlling currency supply and interest rates. Currency is a depreciating asset because it systematically decreases in value as its supply increases year over year.

Inflation happens when there's more money chasing less goods. Over time, more money is required to buy the same goods because inflation erodes the value of currency. Inflation can run at 2%-3% a year and deteriorate purchasing power. In order to *maintain* purchasing power, a 2%-3% return on money is required.

Money doesn't stand still, it's either growing or declining in value. When interest rates are low, purchase things that will increase in value or pay an income. Long-term, equity in publicly traded companies will beat inflation by roughly 7% in inflation adjusted returns. Stocks are good hedges for inflation because company pricing and earnings rise with inflation.

Always consider the inflation adjusted returns on investments. Owning real estate can be a great hedge against inflation. If a house goes up dramatically over 20 years, compare inflation to the home replacement cost. As lumber, building supplies and labor go up each year, so does the price of existing homes.

Building your own business is another good hedge because your customers will have to pay the cost of inflation as the price of your goods, services and labor rise with supply and demand.

The danger of a large net worth not invested to hedge against inflation, is that the original money saved may have half the purchasing power many years later. For example, one million dollars saved may be $500,000 in purchasing power over a 20-year period. This is what happened from 1999 to 2019; gasoline, milk and bread can double in value, but the value of the US dollar can drop by 50%.

The good news is that while the cost of higher education, textbooks, medical care and childcare have gone up faster than inflation, the price of items like televisions, computers, clothing and cell phone plans have decreased. Technology and business efficiency can cause deflation as items become more affordable, but government loans can increase money supply and affect the cost of college education and homes.

Money is a depreciating asset if left alone. Seek a safe place to invest your money so it's hedged against the destructive nature of inflation.

17

THE FLOW OF MONEY

"The whole world is simply nothing more than a flow chart for capital." - Paul Tudor Jones

C apital is constantly flowing from those who know how to manage it to those who don't. Because money is in constant flux, a person that starts out poor in America can end up wealthy, and poor management can erode years of wealth in one generation. No amount of money will overcome consistently bad decisions. In a free market, capitalistic system, money flows towards those that create value and away from those who don't.

- People who risk money too often will lose it to those who know how to protect it.
- Money flows from consumers to business owners of goods and services.
- Money flows to innovative entrepreneurs who create something that's in demand.

- Money flows away from consumers that don't have self-control.
- Money flows to skilled employees that employers need.
- Money flows to innovative businesses and away from outdated, stagnant businesses.
- Money flows to well managed businesses and away from mismanaged ones.
- Money flows from bad professional asset managers to good ones.
- Money flows from bad traders and investors to good ones.

Money is always seeking a good investment. People put money in stocks they think are going up in value. People look to spend money on items and experiences that will make them happy. The key to your financial freedom is finding a way to make money flow in your direction.

- Protect your money from risk.
- Create a business or product that people want and need.
- Practice self-control when purchasing products and services.
- Acquire skills, education and experience to increase earning power.
- Be a creator first and a consumer second.
- Work in industries that are growing and avoid those that are in decline.
- Develop your skills as a good trader or investor.
- Carefully select who manages your money.

The best way to understand the flow of money is the principle of compounding. Compounded money grows exponentially. Returns increase until the compounded returns are greater than the original capital. This is how the rich get richer; the flow of capital doubles and grows exponentially as they create consistent returns. This applies to investment portfolios, traders and businesses or products that consistently return increases on invested capital.

Interest Rate	Years to Double
1%	72
2%	36
3%	24
4%	18
5%	14
6%	12
7%	10.3
8%	9
9%	8
10%	7.2
11%	6.5
12%	6
13%	5.5
14%	5.1
15%	4.8

Another principle applies to the destruction of capital. When money is lost, it sets off a chain of events that are difficult to recover from. If half of the value of a portfolio or a business is lost, it must double in value to get back to even. If a stock falls 50% in value, it must double to get back to even. If a business loses 10% of its sales in a year, it must increase sales by 11% to get back to even. If a business loses 20% of its sales, it takes a 25% increase to get back even. This is why protecting your capital from ruin is so important.

Loss Incurred	Gain Required to Break Even
10%	11.1%
15%	17.7%
20%	25%
25%	33.3%
30%	42.9%
35%	53.9%
40%	66.7%
45%	81.8%
50%	100%
60%	150%
70%	233.3%

The key to financial freedom is to position yourself where the capital is flowing. Be long in the stock market during bull markets, own leading stocks, work at the fastest growing companies, buy houses in growing markets, open a businesses or create online cash flowing assets.

You'll increase your odds of success if you focus your efforts on areas and topics where capital is on the rise. Do research to verify that you're doing the right thing, in the right place and at the right time.

18

UNDERSTANDING MONEY

If you don't fully understand something, keep your money in your pocket until you do.

To make money you must do research, work hard, invest capital and take risks. You should understand the process required to create profits in your field of interest. As a stock trader, I spent years learning every angle of the markets so I could limit my failure and maximize my chance of success. Here are some of things I needed to understand thoroughly before I could invest or trade in the stock market:

- What is a stock?
- How does the stock market work?
- Who's made money in the stock market?
- What was their process?
- How do I buy a stock?
- How do I sell a stock?

- What is commission cost?
- How do commission costs affect my bottom line?
- Is there a way to know if a stock will go up in value?
- How will I lock in profits?
- What are the risks?
- How much money can I make?

I needed to understand these questions before I started trading, but these principles apply to all areas of finance and business. Many people do this backwards; they get excited and rush into a money-making idea without doing the research or having a plan. Whether it's investing, trading, building a business or developing a product, you must do the research on the front end to be successful later.

Ignorance will cost you money, time and happiness. Long-term success comes from study rather than luck, hope or exuberance. Any time you think you have a money-making plan, slow down, sleep on it, research it and make a long-term plan.

Success comes from establishing an edge, and it's important to remember that good opportunities have long shelf lives. Rather than focusing on not missing out on an opportunity, devote your efforts to not wasting money or time.

Confidence should only come after competence. It's expensive to go confidently in the wrong direction.

19

WEALTH PROCESS

"Without wisdom, gold is quickly lost by those who have it, but with wisdom, gold can be secured by those who have it not." - George S. Clason

W ealth is a process that takes time; it's created through the compounded growth of a business, investment or earning power.

Most wealth is generated through risk taking. Risking student loan debt for an education to pursue a high paying career, risking capital in an investment, or risking money to start a business. Typically, the only way to increase the speed of wealth-building is to increase the risk.

Unfortunately, increasing risk is also the fastest way to create a large loss in capital. Consistently looking for ways to grow capital while carefully managing risk is the best path to becoming wealthy. If you continually risk it all, you'll go broke. Never take a risk that will wipe you out the first time you're wrong. No one is right every time.

Egos are expensive in finance, and succumbing to the illusion of getting rich quick can cause you to lose everything. You're asking for trouble if you made money in one area, but expect automatic success in something you're unfamiliar with. It's important to remember that when you change from one area of expertise to another, you will be a beginner until you acquire enough experience to be an expert. That takes time, dedication and practice, and there aren't any shortcuts.

Hope is wonderful. It can get you excited, push you towards your goals and keep you focused on being successful. But it can also blind you when it comes to reason, logic and business math. Hope can give you the inspiration to pursue your dreams, but only the right process will help you fulfill them.

Greed an emotion that hates to wait and wants more than it has earned. Greed causes mistakes because it ignores warning signs, logic and reason. It's important to seek viable ways to speed up financial growth, rather than taking risks that impede success, invite ruin and slow or stop your ability to achieve financial freedom.

20

YOUR FINANCIAL DEFENSE

Insurance is protection against personal ruin.

I nsurance is a tool that allows you to pay a small amount today to avoid the risk of a large loss in the future. Having a large loss can ruin you, and not protecting what you have can make it difficult to compound and grow your net worth. Having insurance can shift what could have been a catastrophe into an inconvenience.

Home insurance isn't optional if you carry a mortgage, but even if your home is paid for, insurance is necessary to avoid the potential of becoming homeless. By paying a relatively small sum every month, you shift the risk to someone else who will pay for your home to be rebuilt if you experience a catastrophic event.

It's necessary to have medical insurance in the US, because one medical emergency could hinder your ability to get sufficient care or lead to bankruptcy. Your medical insurance doesn't have to be tied to your job; you can purchase an individual policy when you decide to work for yourself. Keep in mind that the cost of insurance will likely be at least twice as much as you were paying as an employee, but it's still an important part of protecting your health and personal finances. In most instances, it can be claimed on business taxes if you're self-employed, but make sure you check with your state tax laws before making insurance decisions.

There are many kinds of insurance, and what you have and how much you carry will be a personal decision based on your specific situation. For example, you'll likely need more insurance if you have a family with children in a single family home, than if you're single and live alone in an apartment.

Having the right insurance is an important part of keeping what you've earned while avoiding the risk of ruin.

III

BUILDING WEALTH

21

100% RETURN

Always invest as much as you can in your employer's 401K program, it's free money.

Warren Buffett, George Soros, Paul Tudor Jones and Peter Lynch are some of the best money managers in the world, and even they only see an average of 20% annual returns over long periods. What someone could get a 100% return on their money? This type of return is found in most US employer's 401K programs.

Some people don't know about this benefit, or they don't understand the program's potential and don't participate. A 401K is found in most company benefit packages for full-time employees, and it essentially replaces the defined pension plan program of the last century. Companies created the 401K benefit so they could control their expenses and cap their employee retirement costs. This system replaced the profit sharing program or stock purchase program in some companies.

Instead of putting 10% of an employee's income into a profit sharing account each year, a company could cut their expenses in half by changing to a 401K and matching at 5%. The employee would still receive 10% of their income placed into a tax deferred retirement account, but they would have to contribute the first 5%. Companies save money because most people don't contribute their share, so the employer doesn't have to match anything.

Most major corporations and some private businesses in the US have 401K match programs, and the match criteria will vary. For example, you make $50,000 a year and put 5%, or $50 dollars, into the tax deferred account every week. Your company matches it for a total of $100, which is a 100% return. By the end of the year you will have contributed $2,500 and the company will have contributed $2,500. This is an approximation taking into account a two-week vacation.

Because these plans are typically administered before taxes are taken out of your pay, and you defer taxes until you take the money out, these plans can give you a substantial head start; your seed money can grow tax-free for decades.

Some companies will match the company stock you purchase rather than a percentage of your income. This can also be a good deal because you're buying the stock at half price. You'll have a built-in safety margin, because if the stock drops by 50%, you're still at even. If the stock ends up in a downtrend, you can sell it when the plan permits. The magic happens if you work for a company with good growth and earnings. If you buy stock and your company matches it at 100%, when it doubles, you're up 300%.

Your plan will likely have parameters for how long you must hold the shares after the match. Consider selling the shares when you can, so you don't have as much risk exposure with a lack of diversification. Obviously, this isn't necessarily true if you work for a successful and fundamentally sound company. But if you hold stock in your company, it's important to practice risk management and have an exit strategy to lock in profits or cut losses.

You should get in the habit of automatically deducting your full match from your paycheck into your 401K account. Making enough room in your budget for this habit will take financial discipline and will require you to closely monitor discretionary spending.

Think about it this way, if your new car payment or eating out too often is keeping you from making your full match, then you're paying double for whatever consumer goods you're buying. If your $700 car payment is keeping you from contributing $400 full match each month, then the car is costing you $800 a month in missed opportunity. This is called opportunity cost, and if financial freedom is important to you, you'll learn to say no to expensive goods and services that are sapping your finances and keeping you from making a 100% match.

If you have access to a 401K account through your employer, don't miss out on the best opportunity to get a 100% return on your investment with zero risk. There isn't much free money in the world, so when your employer offers it to you in the form of a 401K retirement program, make it part of your exit strategy.

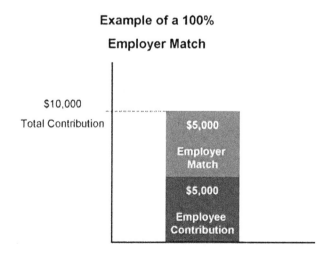

Example of a 100% Employer Match

$10,000
Total Contribution

$5,000
Employer Match

$5,000
Employee Contribution

22

TAXES

"In this world nothing can be said to be certain, except death and taxes." - Benjamin Franklin

---

Depending on where you live, you could be paying up to 100 different taxes. Depending on your income, what you own and how much you spend, it's possible that 50% of your money goes to pay taxes. Here's a list of some taxes you're probably familiar with, and others you may not have thought about.

- Federal income tax
- Corporate income tax
- State income tax
- County tax
- City tax
- Property tax
- Employee and employer social security tax
- Employee and employer Medicare tax

- Unemployment tax
- Sales tax
- Gasoline tax
- Air transportation tax
- Estate tax
- Gift tax
- Wheel tax
- Car registration tax
- Sewer tax
- Mobile phone tax
- 911 emergency tax
- Utility tax
- Corporate and individual dividend tax
- Capital gains tax
- Estate tax

There are more taxes in the form of fines, court fees, speeding tickets, licenses, permits and many more that are embedded in the price you pay.

Taxes are one of the largest expenses in personal finance. Optimizing them to minimize tax liability and keep more of what you earn is one of the most important things you can do financially.

Lower your taxable income by claiming every tax deduction you can, and if you're on the edge of a higher tax bracket, you can save a significant amount of money by investing in deferred retirement accounts like 401Ks, 403Bs and IRAs. You'll eventually have to pay taxes when you withdraw your money, but these accounts do a good job of growing your wealth in a tax-free environment.

Your personal residence is also a good tax haven, and one of the few things that can give you a tax advantage. As long as you've lived in the home long enough, you'll be able to keep the tax-free capital gains after it's sold. This varies by state, as does the amount that's considered tax-free.

An advantage of being a business owner is that the sequence of taxation is different from that of an individual. An employee is issued a paycheck *after* the income tax has been removed, and then pay their expenses with what's left. A business spends money on its expenses *first*, and whatever's left is considered taxable income. If you're employed by a business, they're operating on a better tax structure than you are. For example, when a business buys a new laptop, it's considered to be necessary a necessary investment in the business, and it comes out of company profits *before* taxes are paid. Employees who buy a laptop are doing it with their money *after* it's been taxed.

Likewise, the wealthy also benefit from a better tax structure than employees. Founders and large shareholders of major corporations grow wealthier because they don't have the same tax drag on their money. Many of the richest people in the world like Warren Buffett, Bill Gates and Jeff Bezos have most of their wealth in their company's stock. They pay income tax, dividend tax and capital gains tax, but there isn't (so far) a wealth tax.

The wealthy aren't taxed on their net worth every year, they're only taxed when they have a taxable event. Warren Buffett creates a taxable event when he sells some of his Berkshire-Hathaway stock, if he receives dividends on his shares, or receives pay from being the chairman of Berkshire-Hathaway. There's no taxable event if he holds his shares and doesn't sell them. Billionaires don't pay much in income tax because it's not their income that makes them rich, it's the large amount of stocks they own.

Taxes can diminish your purchasing power. If your income tax rate is 25% and you buy a new car for $30,000, the car actually costs you $40,000 in after tax income. In other words, you must earn $40,000 in income to generate $30,000 in after tax purchasing power. In addition to the sticker price, you must consider the sales tax, wheel tax, registration tax, and all the manufacturing taxes that are passed along to you. When you drive a new car off the lot, it instantly depreciates because you're paying the manufacturing costs. The depreciation includes all the workers' pay, taxes, benefits, manu-facturing costs, transportation costs, research and development, along with advertising and executive pay. When you buy a used car from a seller, you're paying them based only on fair market value.

Each city, county and state have different tax structures. A few states still have no state income taxes, and in these states you're taxed on spending and not earning. If your lifestyle permits, your income isn't location dependent, or you could easily find work in another area, it's worth considering relocating to a tax-free state. Moving to a tax-free state is like giving yourself a large raise.

You may be in a higher tax bracket if you have a family and your spouse works. Calculate all of your expenses, including child care, clothing, cars, gasoline, take-out, etc. Do the math and make sure that it's worth it for both of you to work outside the home; high income earners are taxed heavily, high net worth individuals are not.

23

FORGET THE JONESES

"Loans are what we see: House, car and social media photos of vacations. Wealth is what we don't see: Money in the bank, stocks, and mutual fund balances. Loans make you look rich. Wealth makes you rich." - D. Muthukrishnan

"Keeping up with the Joneses is an idiom in many parts of the English-speaking world referring to the comparison to one's neighbor as a benchmark for social class or the accumulation of material goods. To fail to "keep up with the Joneses" is perceived as demonstrating socio-economic or cultural inferiority." - Wikipedia

Big houses, new cars, lavish vacations and high-powered careers don't equal wealth. If your neighbor drives their new car to a job owned by someone else, it's likely that their boss is the one who's wealthy and they're drowning in debt.

Many people have trouble separating physical items from wealth. Money is wealth and physical items are just things. Studies have shown that many millionaires live ordinary, middle-class lifestyles without flashy cars or big houses. Many of them end up with high net worth and are financially independent because they *aren't* materialistic by nature. People who appear to be wealthy generally fall into one of these financial categories.

- High income earners who own expensive things, have large debt, and low net worth.
- High income earners that live modestly and have high net worth.
- Wealthy people that look upper middle class but have high net worth.
- Ultra-wealthy who live a lavish lifestyles *and* have high net worth.

It's possible to be successful by managing stock option grants, investing in company stock or receiving equity in a young company, but most self-made millionaires own a business and/or are great investors.

There are few employees, no matter how successful, who are wealthy. It's difficult to work for someone else for years, save aggressively and control spending habits enough to be wealthy. If it's accomplished, it's usually more about what they did on the side or how they invested their time, rather than after-tax dollars from a paycheck. And you have to ask yourself, if someone was that successful and comfortable, would they be getting up every morning to go to work for someone else on someone else's terms?

24

CREATING WEALTH

Wealth is created by providing solutions because money flows towards value and creativity.

There are many paths to wealth:

- Enter a trade at the right time and sell it later for a profit.
- Invest in a good company at the right time for the right price and sell it later for a profit.
- Build a business that fulfills customer's needs and they will pay for your goods and services.
- Save part of your income and invest wisely to grow wealth over time.
- Grow wealth by buying real estate in the right place at the right time and sell it for a profit.
- Maximize your time by creating cash flowing assets that continue to generate wealth for years.

- Buy stock option contracts at the right strike price and expiration date and sell at the right time.
- Grow a business and take it through an Initial Public Offering (IPO). If you're able to remain at the company and continue to invest, you'll likely be very wealthy.

The wealthiest people solve the biggest problems. Steve Jobs invented a user friendly, home computer. Bill Gates created software for the home computer. Mark Zuckerberg created the social media platform to connect the world. Sam Walton created the cheapest prices in town. Ray Kroc invented systems for inexpensive fast food.

Capitalism rewards problem solvers by buying their products and investing in their companies. You're rewarded for the size and scope of the problem you solve. You don't have to solve a billion-dollar problem, you just need to solve one big enough to pay for your financial independence.

There are many paths to wealth. It's your job to find the right path for you.

25

STOCK MARKET

Investing in the stock market is one of the best opportunities because you can own a piece of a scalable business without the risk of business ownership.

The stock market is a powerful tool because you don't have to start your own company, you can buy the stock of a successful company run by someone else. The people who invested in Warren Buffett's company, Berkshire-Hathaway, basically hired him to be their business and portfolio manager. This chart demonstrates their success.

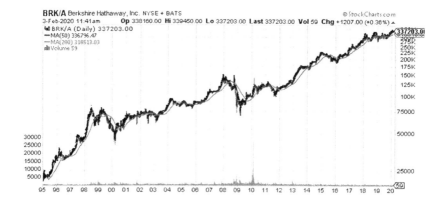

From 2000 to early 2020, Berkshire-Hathaway enjoyed more than a 500% return on their investment, from $50,000 near the bottom, to more than $337,000 in January 2020. Although this is an extreme example and the price was already high in 2000, Buffett started acquiring Berkshire-Hathaway at $7.60 a share in 1962. There were decades of opportunity to invest or trend trade in the company.

If you partner with brilliant business minds who produce quality goods and services, you can reap the benefits of their success. Jeff Bezos made many of his investors wealthy on his way to becoming the richest man in the world. The world's richest people typically increase the share price of the publicly traded companies they own, and you can join them on their ascent.

Too many people spend their lives as employees and consumers, selling their time and skill for money, while overlooking opportunities to become investors. This mentality insures that you stay on the consumer side of a company and the never ending treadmill of work and spend. Buying products from Amazon is spending money, buying shares of Amazon stock is investing money.

Customers spend money to consume goods and services that depreciate, while investors spend money to accumulate assets that can appreciate over time. The best performing stocks of all-time were not obscure penny stocks, biotech names or secret insider picks. They were household names like Wal-Mart, Apple, Home Depot, Price-line, Google, Intel, Cisco, Microsoft, Amazon and Netflix.

A company needs growth in their business model to see the stock price increase. This growth happens by building a large customer base and providing goods and services that those customers find valuable. Good opportunities for investment are hard to miss, and you may find the best opportunities while shopping online or in your neighborhood. In addition to finding the right company, you must buy at the right price, and the stock should be in a stable price range or uptrend.

Things to consider before investing in a company include profit margins, competitive advantage, industry and growth prospects. There are also technical aspects of stock price. Is it a good price for entry? Is it a value at that price? Is future growth already priced in? Is the chart pattern of the stock bullish or bearish? Is price in an uptrend or downtrend? Is there a safety margin at that price, and how much lower could it go?

Many people have tight budgets, but it's crucial that you start saving and investing for the future. Even a small investment, like $100 a month into your savings account is a step in the right direction. Your money can be placed in a brokerage account, individual retirement account, 401K or 403B. It's a good idea to have a tax deferred account if you don't plan on touching the money for a decade or more.

If you're doing short term speculating and trading, then a brokerage account is needed. Brokerage accounts are quick and easy to open online, and most major stock brokers offer zero commissions. Make sure that your broker has trading fees that are under $10. Your first account can be used to speculate in pursuit of short term returns, or an account you plan to use long-term for retirement; keep in mind that people typically have both account types.

Turning earned income into ownership of equity in the best, publicly traded companies is one of the best paths to financial independence. This is a short overview of the power of trading. For more in-depth explanations of trading and investing, visit our other book titles on Amazon or our eCourses at New Trader University.

26

HOME OWNERSHIP

Investing in a home can be a path to building wealth, but it's critical that you understand what you can afford and live within your means.

In Thomas Stanley's book, *The Millionaire Next Door,* he recommends that the cost of a new home is less than double your annual income. If your family income is $150,000 a year, you should buy a home for less than $300,000. If you want a larger home, then you need to increase your income. If you buy a house that's beyond your means, the mortgage will put a drain on your finances and you won't be able to invest enough money to become financially independent. It's that simple.

Remember that the mortgage may be just the beginning of your expenditures. You must have enough money leftover after paying your mortgage to pay for the expenses associated with home ownership, like replacing HVAC units or roofs.

One of the best ways to save, especially when starting out with your first home, is to buy a new build that meets the income-to-house ratio rule above. A new build will give you 10-15 years with minimal maintenance expenses, and if you buy a home from a reputable builder in a growing area, your home could become an important appreciable asset.

Debt isn't dangerous if managed correctly and used as a tool to help you achieve your goals. If you use debt to buy consumer goods that go down in value, you're taking on large risks and making it difficult to obtain financial independence. The best use of debt is buying things that can go up in value like a home or a business. If you take out a 15-year mortgage on a house that costs $300,000 and it goes up an average of 2% per year, you're increasing your net worth by $6,000 per year after financing fees and mortgage interest.

When you first obtain a mortgage, you may not be net positive, but your annual interest is reduced each year as you pay your principal on the mortgage amortization table. Your equity accrues as the value of your home increases. If your home increases by $6,000 a year, in 10 years you have over $60,000 in equity before the compounded growth year over year. After 10-years in a 15 year mortgage, you'll only have a few years left to pay on your home, and the odds are that you'll soon have a six-figure net worth. After your home is paid for in 15 years, you'll be living mortgage and rent free, giving you more money to invest in your future.

It's also important to acknowledge that you have to live somewhere, and one of the best reasons to get a mortgage is that it's a hedge against inflation. A mortgage locks in monthly housing expenses, while rent can increase every time you sign a new lease. Remember that a personal residence is federal tax-free capital gains when you sell it in the US, up to a point. Check with the your state's tax laws for more information on their regulations.

The zip code you buy a home in makes a difference. Buy in areas that are growing and not declining and avoid zip codes that are over-priced. Consider areas that are less expensive if your job isn't location dependent. You'll save money and likely get twice the house and land if you're willing to live further from large cities.

While home ownership can be a good thing, it's not for everyone. Some digital nomads live frugally while traveling the world and wouldn't have it any other way. Others prefer to rent so they don't have unexpected home ownership expenses. The most important thing is that you love where you live and that it fits in with your financial goals. Your house can either be your biggest asset or the biggest drain on your ability to create wealth.

27

RISK AND REWARD

"It's not whether you're right or wrong, but how much money you make when you're right and how much you lose when you're wrong." - George Soros

All areas of your life are full of risk and reward, and it's important to be aware of both sides before making large life decisions. The maximum risk in any situation is how much you can lose in a worst-case scenario. The reward is the maximum you receive if everything goes according to plan.

If a decision doesn't work out, the downside can be lost capital, increased debt or bankruptcy. If the decision goes your way, you can make substantial amounts of money. The key to successful finances is making good bets when the odds are in your favor. Mark Zuckerberg had little risk when he started programming Facebook in his dorm room. If it didn't work he would continue attending Harvard, but if his idea was successful, he could become one of the richest people in the world.

A Warren Buffett principle of success is buying great companies at prices that have a good risk/reward ratio. The upside of the growth potential far outweighs the risk of failure. If he buys a company's stock at $30 a share and it has the potential to grow by ten times, he's only risked $30 to make $300. The upside potential is unlimited and his downside is minimal, because the maximum risk is usually a 50% drop in price. This is considered to be an asymmetrical investment because the reward is much greater than the risk. Much of the world's wealth is acquired by asymmetrical investing.

The best time to find your passion and follow it is when you're young, single and just starting out. By the time you have a family, a mortgage and a lot of monthly bills, you may have locked yourself into a lifestyle that you can't easily replace if you choose to, or have to, leave your job.

Start when you're young and build on what you want to do long-term until you can transition to living your dream full-time. And always carefully consider the risk and the reward of any financial decision.

28

KNOWLEDGE AND SKILL

"Ultimately, there's one investment that supersedes all others: Invest in yourself. Nobody can take away what you've got in yourself, and everybody has potential they haven't used yet." -
Warren Buffett

Increasing your skillset and improving your mindset is the best investment you can make. Improving yourself makes you more valuable as an employee, business owner or investor. Every book you read, every technical skill you learn, every class or seminar you take can put money in your pocket. People pay for value, and value comes from the critical thinking necessary to utilize knowledge in a way that can be monetized.

As you gain experience in a specific area, you'll become more valuable because you'll have knowledge of what works and what doesn't, and that wisdom can positively affect the operation of a company. The best jobs are those that increase your knowledge and skills, because you're getting paid to learn and grow. If a high paying job is part of your financial independence plan, then you must have knowledge and skills that are in demand to receive a larger paycheck. If you want to start a business, then learning about management, production and the profit and loss statements is crucial to your success.

There are many ways to acquire the knowledge and skills necessary, and you'll need spend time aligning them with your goals. This will help you decide how much formal education you need, whether you can learn through mentorship, or whether you can learn what you need to know from books or workshops. Whatever path you take, try to carve out an hour every day to read a book that motivates you and increases your knowledge.

IV

FINANCIAL FREEDOM

29

FIRING YOUR BOSS

"How in the hell could a man enjoy being awakened at 8:30 a.m. by an alarm clock, leap out of bed, dress, force-feed, shit, piss, brush teeth and hair, and fight traffic to get to a place where essentially you made lots of money for somebody else and were asked to be grateful for the opportunity to do so? " - Charles Bukowski

When I post a message about people being financially independent, it's typically met with a negative or incredulous reply. Many people demand to know what would happen if *everyone* quit their jobs. They're convinced that the economy would collapse if everyone followed my advice.

The reality is that most people won't try to be entrepreneurs or seek financial independence because few will seriously consider working for themselves. Some won't know that it's possible or how to do it. Many won't have the desire to study, work hard and invest the capital necessary for success. It's easier for some people to live a passive lifestyle; watching television, working for someone else for a paycheck and going into debt to keep up with societal norms.

These people are necessary for the economy to function, and they should be appreciated for the work they're willing to do every day. For many of them, they're living their best life, with a job they love, a boss that respects them and co-workers that they consider second family. However, for people who don't love what they do or who they work for, there are alternatives.

We live in a free country. You can choose to live and work where you would like. If you're unhappy with your current employment and you're unable to go out on your own or retire, then find another job. Don't fall into the trap of thinking, *what if the next job is worse.* There's risk when you make a change, but ask yourself *what if it's much, much better?*

Have you ever considered why people who leave unhealthy or unhappy work environments use the word *quitting*? It makes it sound like they're an undisciplined slacker who's giving up without cause, rather than someone moving on to find a better work environment. Just like you can be fired as an employee, you should feel like you can fire your boss for not meeting your needs or expectations.

Obviously, you need to be prepared if you want to fire your boss and do something else. If you're going to continue to be an employee, start looking for employment with another company in your industry and try to upgrade your pay or benefits in the process. If you're able to downsize your house, cars and unnecessary debt before making the switch, you'll be that much better off in the long-term. And it may be a good time to start thinking about a side-hustle that could bring in extra money or create a path to self-employment.

Reasons to fire your boss:

- You're consistently unhappy and dread going to work
- Your pay doesn't reflect what's expected of you
- Your job has no respect for your personal time
- The job environment is unhealthy

- The job negatively affects your personal relationships
- There are better opportunities for you to pursue
- Your career has stagnated and there's no upward mobility or chance of promotion
- The company's long-term prospects aren't good

One of the downsides of being an employee is that you have no income diversification; your boss is the primary decision maker when it comes to your financial security. As a business owner, you'll likely have customers who take the place of your boss, and this is a better risk reward ratio than having all of your eggs in your boss's basket.

How fast you can find another way to pay bills determines how much leverage your boss has over you. The more financial security you have, the more your boss will need to worry about keeping their job as your employer. Remember, you can start interviewing new bosses anytime.

30

YOUR JOURNEY

"Those who don't have debt have more choices in life. Debt cripples our freedom." - D. Muthukrishnan

---

I often share my experiences and opinions about financial freedom on social media, and I frequently receive comments that disagree with my philosophy.

- *You can't take it with you so you might as well enjoy it now.*
- *I could never quit my job, how would I pay my bills?*
- *I want to travel and enjoy life now when I'm in good health.*

Most of these responses come from a predetermined belief system, and instead of listening with an open mind and imagining a different life, they become defensive or hostile.

It's true that you can't take material things with you, but if one of your main motivations is the acquisition of items, you'll have the potential for greater purchasing power if you're financially independent. Remaining an employee for the rest of your life guarantees that you'll never get ahead. You'll go into debt to buy something, hope it's paid for by the time you need to replace it, and start over or add more debt when you get a new one.

Early investors in leading companies, millionaire traders that compound their capital, and profitable business owners are able to purchase what they want *and* have time to enjoy their success. Working towards financial freedom doesn't mean you have to live without creature comforts. Your desire for financial freedom will be evident by your level of personal commitment, self-control, and your ability to focus on more than owning material goods.

The first step is finding something you're passionate about so you can get started making the sacrifices and putting in the hard work necessary to be successful. You'll find that if you do something you're passionate about, you'll work 10x harder than you ever did for someone else and you'll love doing it.

It's possible to enjoy life while building your future. Enjoy the process of working hard every day on something you're passionate about. Relish the fact that you're making your own schedule, playing by your own rules and being your own boss. Having the freedom to set your own priorities and directly affect your success will give you just as much satisfaction as a new car, big house or a tropical vacation. The good news is that you can have all of those things, too! The harder you work for yourself the more successful you'll be, and what you do with that success is up to you.

Financial freedom isn't necessarily about being frugal, it's about doing things in the correct order. Create the life you want with adequate cash flow first, then buy things that give you pleasure. Don't go into debt for things you can't afford today or you'll end up trapped in a job when the bill comes due tomorrow. Try to make a point to enjoy the journey *and* the destination.

31

YOUR OPPORTUNITY

"He who works all day has no time to make money." - John D. Rockefeller

The means of industrial production is no longer controlled by a few capitalists like it was 150 years ago. The barriers to entry have changed, monopolies are being broken and the new economy is being built on platforms that anyone can utilize and monetize.

- Amazon is open to outside sellers, publishers and authors.
- AirBnB makes it possible for anyone to own a rental property.
- Uber has removed barriers for ride-share drivers and revolutionized personal travel.
- Apple is open to musicians, publishers and game developers.

- YouTube is a multimedia platform for creators around the world.
- Anyone can create and monetize a blog or website.
- Social media platforms allow everyone to advertise as equals.
- Facebook allows you to be friends with and learn from people you would otherwise never know.
- Instagram lets you share your ideas and creativity with the world for free.
- Online learning has lowered the barrier to entry in most fields.
- 3D printers allow people to create products without a factory or inventory.
- Etsy and Shopify allow anyone to open their own eCommerce store.
- Professional trading and investing tools are now available to anyone for free.

Financial freedom is about benefitting from the economic value that you create. Be your own boss and cut out the middlemen that benefit from your labor without adding to your personal bottom line.

32

YOUR RETIREMENT

Your goal should not be a job, your goal should be your long-term financial security.

M any aspire to get a good job and a steady paycheck, while others dream of starting their own business and being their own boss. Whatever your goals, it's important to start your journey as early as possible with the end game in mind.

Do you want to work for someone else and earn a steady paycheck? Do you have a business idea? Do you have a hobby that you can monetize? Do you want to retire early and travel the world? It's important to ask yourself *why* you're working. Even if you're most interested in the security of working for someone else, you need to consider that your health, personal emergencies or the economy may change your plans; it's important to have a backup plan.

Regardless of your long-term financial goals, it's imperative that you become fiscally responsible as soon as possible. Focus on turning your earned income into investments, cash flowing assets and paying off debt.

Maximize any benefits that you have access to, like 401K, stock options and discounted stock purchases. The sooner you get started, the more your capital can compound and the quicker you will be financially independent.

The number of years that you can work are limited, but your expenses are forever. Income rarely keeps up with housing expenses, medical costs and the cost of living. Start thinking about your retirement as early as possible. You may retire in your 30s or 70s, depending on your income, financial habits and investments. Retirement can be wonderful or stressful depending on how early you start planning for it.

What you do in retirement is up to you, and there's no reason that retiring from an employer can't mean starting your own business. Don't think of it as a time of rocking chairs and doing nothing (unless that's what you want to do), think of it as the beginning of the next chapter of your life.

33

YOUR PATH

You don't have to rely on a job to make money, look for other paths that will lead to your goal.

Most people think the only way to make money is to go to college and get a good job. This is one path to financial freedom, but it's just one of many. There's nothing wrong with a job, but don't limit yourself to a single source of income or one path to financial independence. Increase your ability to create cash flowing assets and you'll increase your net worth and your opportunities.

- Actively trading financial markets for capital gains can create compounded financial growth. Six years of 20% annual returns can double your money.
- Investing in a stock market index ETF through buy and hold investing grows capital at an average rate of 10% a year.

- Investing in the right stock can turn thousands of dollars into millions over a few decades.
- You can own stocks that pay you a share of the company's earnings through dividends.
- You can own a bond that pays you interest for lending the bond seller money with your purchase.
- Buying a cash flowing asset like a rental property, vending machine, car wash, laundry mat, etc., can make you money while you sleep.
- Create cash flowing assets like books, websites, eCommerce stores, YouTube channels or eCourses.
- You can purchase an owner operator franchise or purchase a business and hire someone else to run it for you.
- You can create your own business by providing a service directly to customers.
- You can own a home that goes up in value.
- You can own commercial real estate that you lease to businesses.

Creating multiple streams of income creates financial peace of mind, diversifies risk and increases your net worth.

34

YOUR FREEDOM

"He who works all day, has no time to make money" - John
Rockefeller

Many people worry about what they'll do if they gain financial
independence. It can be scary to be the captain of your own
ship. The loss of regimented structure designed by others can be
disconcerting, especially in the beginning. It's important to focus on
the positive aspects of your new life.

You now have control of your schedule based on your personal
habits and productivity. Some people work better in the morning and
prefer to get up early and end their day early. Others prefer to start
later in the day and work into the night. Working based on the
schedule that's most comfortable for you is rarely an option when you
work for someone else. It's important to keep a schedule and maximize productivity, but now you can do makes the most sense for you,
your family and your business.

Some people feel guilty about working for themselves on their own terms, because society has instilled a sense of guilt about it. This is especially true if you don't have to work every day or rely on income from cash flowing assets. It can be difficult for people to separate work from money, and to realize that for many cash flowing assets, you do a lot of work upfront so you can reap the benefits for years. If you plant a fruit tree and care for it until maturity, you can enjoy the fruit for years with minimal effort; you don't have to plant a new fruit tree every day.

If you've been working on a side business or investing part-time, it will be much easier to make money faster when you're able to dedicate your full attention and efforts to your financial independence.

It's a wonderful feeling when your hard work and dedication culminates in financial freedom. You can take time to create, relax, start a new hobby, spend time with your family and enjoy your new life. What can you do when you achieve financial freedom? Whatever you want to do.

35

YOUR TIME

"Financial independence not only allows you to control your own time, it also helps you to buy others time. Time is the most finite and precious wealth." - D. Muthukrishnan

Most people go through life mindlessly buying products and going on vacations because they work for someone else and accept a paycheck in return for their time. Few people realize that with a few changes to their habits and lifestyle, they could buy back their time and put it to work for them.

You need a job because you have monthly bills and you need a regular paycheck to pay those bills, but how much is your time worth? How much would you pay to have access to all the hours you spend working for someone else? When you considering this question, remember to add up the commute time, business travel, meals away from home, etc.

Don't underestimate the value of your time. When you have the ability to reclaim it, you'll be able to use your creativity and energy to work on things that you're passionate about or give you joy. Would you write a book or start a website? Would you start a podcast or a YouTube channel? Do you have a hobby that you can monetize with an eCommerce site? Anything is possible when you have the energy and time to work on something you're passionate about.

Escaping the grind and taking back your time allows you to turn off your ringer and decompress. It gives you the ability to save money and get healthier. It keeps you from spending money on things you wouldn't ordinarily need to purchase like gasoline to commute. More importantly, buying back your time allows you to live a more balanced life with friends and family. Ask yourself what dollar amount you put on your quality of life.

Become financially independent and wake up when you want, take a day off when you want, build what you want, dress how you want and be who you want.

Time is your most important asset because it's a nonrenewable asset. Everyone only has 24 hours in a day, and a life span of about 80 years if they're lucky. Having ownership of your time and being able to do what you want to do is the best investment you can make.

36

YOUR FOCUS

"The best thing money can buy is neither possessions nor experiences, but freedom." - D. Muthukrishnan

---

A luxury item is a product that's desirable but not a necessity. Luxury items are typically acquired by wealthy people who have expendable income and want the best money can buy or to show their social status. Having expensive items may be nice, but nothing compares to having financial freedom.

Would you rather own an expensive house that you have to leave for 40 to 60 hours a week while you work for someone else, or have a home you can payoff and enjoy all day, every day? Would you rather drive a luxury car on your one-hour commute, or have a paid off, used car in your driveway while you commute from your kitchen to your home office? Would you rather enjoy a one-week lavish vacation to an exotic destination, or make every day a vacation because you have no job to get away from?

Financial freedom is about freedom from the obligation to earn a paycheck. It's about having enough space between your bills and your income to live stress-free.

Financial freedom is the ultimate luxury item, because it alleviates the pressures of working for someone else, constantly grinding away on the treadmill of consumerism, in a world that treats you like a number.

There's more to life than working for someone else, letting them benefit from your labor, skills, experience and ideas. Achieving financial freedom gives you choices. It gives you peace of mind and gives you the opportunity to do something you're passionate about. It helps you live a balanced life and spend more time with your family and friends. How fast you get there, and what you do when you get there, will be up to you.

If you stay focused on your goals and committed to your success, only time will separate you from achieving financial freedom.

EPILOGUE

People struggle with the idea of working for themselves, but there are more ways than ever before to make a living without reporting to a boss. It may be necessary to work for someone else when you're just getting started, depending on your background and personal situation, but it doesn't have to be a permanent solution.

All jobs in the private sector come from businesses that were started by someone with a passion. Instead of trading your time for a paycheck with that company, you could trade the company's stock or choose to be inspired by their success and start your own business.

A common misconception is that the financially independent sit on a beach sipping frozen drinks and never work again. I can't tell you how many times people ask me, *"What do you do all day?"* Your still working when you transition into a full-time trader, investor, self-employed business owner, author or real estate investor. The difference is that you're working for *yourself* doing something that you're passionate about; that's the power of financial freedom.

With freedom comes responsibility. You must have the work ethic to be your own boss, the ability to hold yourself accountable and the drive and dedication to be successful. When you work for yourself, you trade a steady paycheck for the irregular income of the profits your business can generate. You move from a fixed salary predetermined by someone else, to the unlimited potential determined by your dedication and hard work.

Money isn't random, it has principles and rules that govern what happens. Regardless of where you start in life, there are ways that you can create positive cash flow and become financially independent. It's important to look for ways to start trading comfort for opportunity and leisure time for productivity as you begin your journey toward financial freedom. You don't need enough money to do nothing, you just need enough money to do whatever you want.

Hopefully this book has given you some things to think about and will help you on your journey. We hope that you will soon experience the peace, joy and fulfillment that comes from financial freedom.

Steve and Holly Burns
New Trader U Blog
New Trader U eCourses

READY TO TAKE YOUR TRADING TO THE NEXT LEVEL?

Join thousands of other trading students at New Trader University! Our eCourses are created especially for those just starting out in the markets.

New Trader 101

The place to start for new traders! Become successful with less stress. In the New Trader 101 eCourse, you'll get:

- 13 high quality videos covering how and why to trade
- Real trade examples with detailed charts
- The most powerful trading psychology and stress management techniques being offered today.

Join New Trader 101 today!

Moving Averages 101

Everything you need to know to harness the power of Moving Averages! In the Moving Averages 101 eCourse, you'll get:

- 11 high quality videos covering how to get started with Moving Averages
- Real trade examples
- More than 45 annotated charts

Join Moving Averages 101 today!

Price Action Trading 101

Master the concepts of reactive technical analysis and learn the best times to get in and out of your trades! In the Price Action Trading 101 eCourse, you'll get:

- 17 high quality videos covering the best way to enter and exit your trades for a profit.
- Step-by-step examples
- More than 30 annotated charts

Join Price Action Trading 101 today!

Options 101

This 19-part video course is packed with information about Options, and how they can help you up your trading game. It includes real trading examples, many visuals, and an Options Play Strategy Guide that you won't find anywhere else. In the Options 101 eCourse, you'll get:

- 19 high quality videos covering how and why to trade
- Step-by-step trading examples
- Many annotated charts

Join Options 101 today!

Real Trade Examples: Volume 1

Have you ever wanted to have a private consultation with Steve? To see how and why he trades the way he does? This is your chance at a fraction of the cost of a one-on-one consultation. Steve will show you step-by-step how he enters, when he exits, and the signals that he follows for maximum profitability.

These 19 real trade examples have interactive, annotated charts and downloadable PDFs that you can use to take your own trading to the next level!

Join Real Trade Examples: Volume 1 today!

Did you enjoy this eBook?

Please consider writing a review.

Listen to many of our titles on Audio!

Read more of our bestselling titles:

New Trader Rich Trader (Revised and Updated)

Moving Averages 101

So You Want to be a Trader

New Trader 101

Moving Averages 101

Buy Signals and Sell Signals

Trading Habits

Investing Habits

Calm Trader